3D ORIGAMI

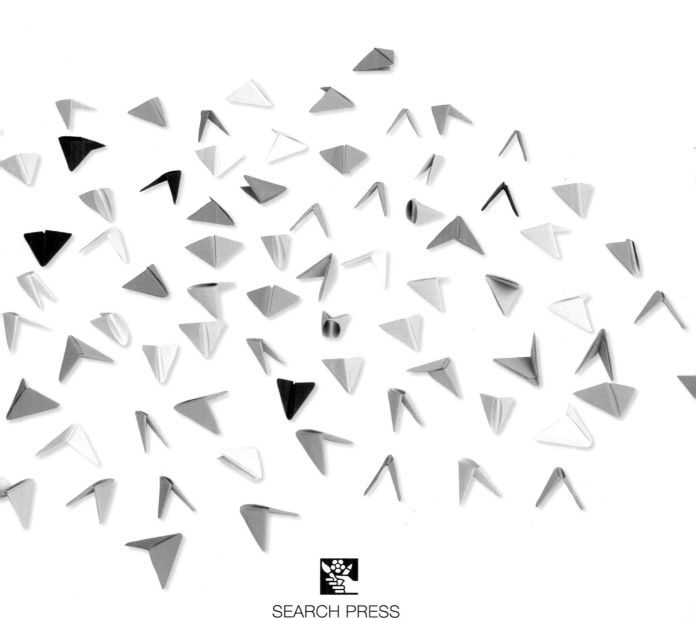

SEARCH PRESS

This book is dedicated to all those who love art and find within it a way of expressing their own love of life.

A special thanks to Colorificio Cadorna for all the materials provided.

First published in Great Britain in 2016
by Search Press Limited, Wellwood,
North Farm Road, Tunbridge Wells, Kent TN2 3DR

Original Italian title published as
Origami A Moduli Triangolari in 2013
by Il Castello

Copyright © 2013 Il Castello srl, via Milano 73/75,
20010 Cornaredo (Mi), Italy

English translation by Burravoe Translation Services

Typesetting by Greengate Publishing Services

ISBN: 978-1-78221-409-0

Printed in China

3D ORIGAMI

Maria Angela Carlessi

CONTENTS

PREFACE

'The world can only be created through passion.'

My name is Maria Angela Cadessi. I do not write professionally, but as a hobby. I became interested in 3D origami by chance; I was looking for a new hobby to suggest to my customers (I have an artist's supply shop, selling all kinds of arts and crafts materials) and I came across a swan created using this technique: I was fascinated. As I couldn't find books written in my own language on the subject, I found it extremely difficult to learn, but hard work paid off and the result is this manual that was intended to be a tribute to the beauty of the works of art created by the Japanese. For origami is an ancient art that originated in Japan, which once seemed an inaccessible country. In the modern world, distances are much shorter, and we are all more familiar with Japanese culture.

The 3D origami technique does not require special skills, merely a bit of patience. The initial folding must be very accurate: speed in execution comes with time and practice. Each project comes with detailed explanations to allow the work to be carried out easily.

By following my advice, I am sure that you will enjoy excellent results, and will, in time, be able to create subjects of your own design.

Enjoy yourselves!

Maria Angela Cadessi

MATERIALS

Paper

The paper, which can be bought in hobby and craft shops, is the essential part of the work. It needs to be pliable, strong, smooth and light and must not lose shape during folding. Flimsy paper or card cannot be used because they do not provide the right hold between one triangle and the next. It is worth taking care over your paper selection, as unsuitable paper will affect the final result. Also pay attention to your choice of colours, as the right combination plays an important role in the projects. The triangles used in this book are obtained from 8 × 4cm (3¼ × ⅝in) rectangles. If you want to reduce the size of the model, you will need to create smaller triangles, using smaller paper rectangles; conversely, if you want to increase the size of your model, you will need to use larger rectangles.

Foam sheets

Rubber foam in pressed sheets is available in different thicknesses and colours. In this book, it is used to create details such as beaks and wings. You can replace it with card, but the result will be less soft and elegant.

Felt

This material is created from felted wool (also available in a synthetic version), and is available in different thicknesses and colours. It can be found in hobby and craft shops.

Eyes and noses

These can be found ready-made in various shapes and sizes, with fixed or mobile pupils.

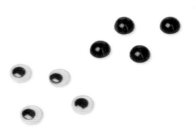

TECHNIQUE

Folding the triangles

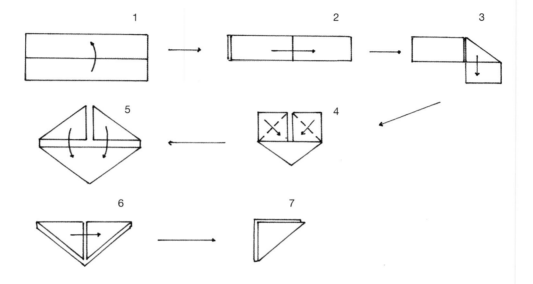

Folding the paper is not only the most important phase of the work but also the longest. We recommend you prepare enough triangles to complete the project before you begin. The paper must be cut into rectangles and the longest side must be twice the length of the shortest side. I normally use 8 × 4cm (3¼ × ⅝in) rectangles, but you can use smaller or larger rectangles depending on the size of the work you want to make.

To create the triangle, fold the paper sheet in half along its length (1), then fold in half along its width to mark the fold line (2). Press down on the edges with your thumbnail, unfold and then fold the right side down to the bottom (3). Do the same with the left side. Then turn the piece over and fold in the two flaps, leaving a few millimetres (4–5). Continue by folding the paper in half (6) and then in half again (7).

Basic rules for folding paper:

a) Fold slowly on a firm, flat surface.

b) Fold carefully and accurately.

c) Go over each fold with your thumbnail.

READING THE PATTERNS

You will see the photograph of the finished model at the beginning of each project and next to it the materials you will need to create it. Please note that the number of triangles needed for the project is always rounded up in excess, as a few pieces may be spoiled when you are making the model.

Wherever possible, the projects are accompanied by a table like the one shown below:

Row	1–2	3	4	5	6	7	8
Light blue	30	15	6	5 × 2	6 + 3 + 2	30 reverse	
White		15	5	5 × 2	5 + 4 + 2		
Blue			19	10	2 + 5		30

Row: shows the row being worked on. Usually, when you see '1–2', this means that the two rows are connected (see *Opening technique,* page 10), which often happens at the beginning of a project. In later rows, when you find, for example, '3–8', this means that the same row should be repeated until you reach row 8 (in this case, row 3,4,5,6,7,8).

The colour: indicates the colour to be used in the various rows.

The number beneath each row number: indicates the number of triangles to be used in each colour.

Each row must be read from top to bottom. For example:

- Row 1–2: use thirty light-blue triangles for row 1 and thirty for row 2.
- Row 3: use fifteen light-blue triangles and fifteen white triangles.
- Row 4: use six light-blue triangles, then five white and then nineteen blue ones.
- Row 5: use five light-blue triangles, then five white and then ten blue ones; 'x 2' means that you have to repeat twice, so you need to use another five light-blue and then five white.
- Row 6: use six light-blue, then five white, then two blue; next use three light-blue, four white and five blue; then continue with two light-blue and two white, all on the same row.

- Row 7: number thirty is followed by the word 'reverse'. This means that you have to use thirty light-blue triangles reversed (see *Straight and reverse triangles*, page 12).
- Row 8: the number thirty on the blue line means that you have to use thirty blue triangles.

N.B. All the work is carried out with the straight triangles.

Otherwise:

- The word 'reverse' next to the number will be present if it only changes for that line.
- The word 'reverse' will be at the beginning of the instructions, before the table, when it continues for several lines.

OPENING TECHNIQUE

After folding the triangles, almost all the projects begin in the way described below; in just a few cases a different technique is used (see *Creating a closed base*, page 16).

Examine your triangles (see page 12). Each one opens out into two wings or points. On the back, or spine, of each triangle you will find two pockets. Slip the right-hand point of one triangle into the left-hand pocket of another to join them. The first two rows are always connected together because otherwise it would not be possible to join the triangles.

Continue by inserting the left-hand point of a new triangle into the right-hand pocket of the previous triangle shown below.

Insert all the triangles shown in the table in rows '1–2' in this way. Check that the first and last triangles are positioned correctly so that they can be inserted into each other.

Join the first triangle with the last to form a circle. Place the circle on a flat surface and check that all the connections are correct and placed properly. This completes rows 1 and 2.

Now continue with row 3 and insert a new red triangle over two yellow triangle points, and repeat this all the way around until the entire row is completed.

To make the circular shape, squeeze the points between your hands as if to close them (do this gently, otherwise you risk ripping the paper). Wait until you have completed four or five rows before doing this so that you can shape the model properly.

STRAIGHT AND REVERSE TRIANGLES

The triangles that you have prepared are all the same, but will produce a different effect depending on whether they are used straight or reverse.

To tell the difference, just look at your triangle:

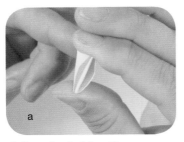

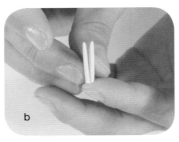

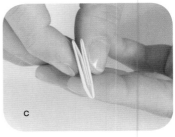

a) One short side with two pockets.

b) The other short side with two points.

c) A longer side with two double returning points.

The side with the two pockets (a) is the place where the triangle points should be inserted. If you insert with the longer side on top, your work is straight. If you insert with the longer side on the bottom, your work will be reverse.

Straight

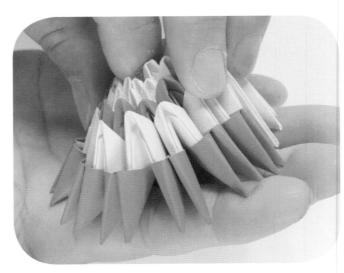

Reverse

INCREASING AND DECREASING TRIANGLES

Increasing

Increases can be made in different ways depending on the model you are making. To increase the number of triangles in a round shape, hook the first new triangle onto one point (normally you would put a triangle onto two points at once) and insert another new triangle on the second point.

To increase the triangles on a flat base, insert a new triangle into the space between two triangles. Secure it then with a triangle on the next row.

Repeat to secure the second point of the new triangle.

By continuing for the entire circle, you will enlarge the circumference of the round shape.

If you want to create a swan's wing, for example, to increase its volume, insert a triangle on the final point, keeping the pocket empty on the inside.

In the next row, hook a triangle onto an additional one and insert a new triangle on the last free point.

Continue for each row, always inserting a new triangle on the last point, to create a fan shape.

Decreasing

To reduce the number of triangles, slip two points into one pocket and one point into the next one.

CREATING A CLOSED BASE

Take a triangle and put the left-hand pocket of one onto the right-hand point of the other. Continue, inserting the left-hand point of a new triangle into the right-hand pocket of the previous one.

Now take a new reverse triangle and insert the two points into the central pockets below, pushing upwards.

Continue by taking a new triangle and putting the left-hand pocket onto the right-hand point. Carry on, inserting the left-hand point of a new triangle into the right-hand pocket of the previous one.

Again take a new reverse triangle and insert the two points into the central pockets below, pushing upwards. Continue until you have used all the triangles for that row.

Bring the two ends together to create the circle and insert a reverse triangle into the remaining pockets to close it.

To create a closed base, you will need to calculate the size of the triangles to be inserted below. For a base beginning with eighteen triangles, use paper measuring 8 × 4cm (3¼ × ⅝in); for a base using twenty-six triangles, use paper measuring 8 × 6cm (3¼ × 2½in) (this is the only case where one measurement is not twice the other measurement). Try the measurement on a circular-shaped piece you have already created, bearing in mind the circle's radius.

CREATING LONG ELEMENTS

These techniques will be used each time you need to create a long, thin element, such as the swan's neck, or arms or a tail.

The first, most simple technique involves inserting one triangle into another several times, and then giving it the desired shape.

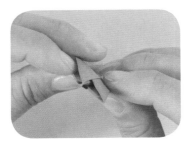
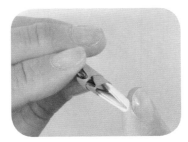

In the second technique shown below, which is a little more complex, you take a triangle and insert another triangle onto each of its points.

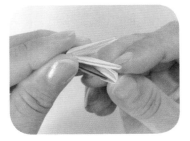

Hook another new triangle over it, creating a bird-foot shape with four points.

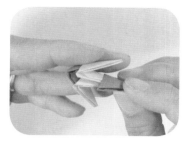 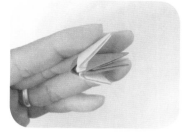

Continue by hooking a triangle over the two centre points. Now slip a new triangle over one point from the previous row and one from the most recently inserted triangle. Repeat on the other side. Continue by inserting a new triangle in the middle.

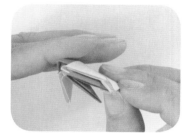  

Repeat these two operations several times, until you reach the desired length.

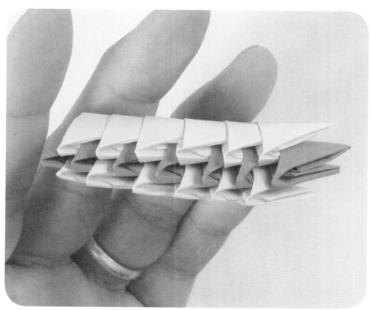

THE PROJECTS
Swan

Materials required:

460 dark-blue triangles

135 light-blue triangles

115 white triangles

Glue

Black marker pen

Transparent matt protective spray

Prepare the triangles as explained in the *Technique* section (page 8), taking care with the folds. Continue with the rows as described in *Opening technique* (page 10).

Row	1–2	3	4	5	6	7	8
Dark blue	30	30		30		30	
White					30		
Light blue			30				30

Front part

As the work has been all the same up to this point, start from any point on the circle and begin from row 9.

Row	9	10	11	12	13	14
Light blue	6	5	4	3	2	1

Position one dark-blue triangle on the left-hand side of the light-blue triangles you have just slotted in and continue upwards, taking one dark-blue triangle together with the point of the one placed previously. Once you reach the top, proceed in the same way on the right-hand side. Insert one dark-blue triangle on the top. Start from the bottom with one dark-blue triangle and continue upwards as in the previous round, both left and right, and end by leaving the two triangles on the top.

Back part

For the back part, work with reverse triangles. From the front, leave four points and begin with row 9 (if the piece is correct, after placing the triangles from row 9, there should be four points on the right and four to the left).

Row	9	10	11	12	13	14
Dark blue	16	15 + 1 + 1	16 + 1 + 1	17 + 1 + 1	18 + 1 + 1	19 + 1 + 1

From row 16, begin to increase the triangles on the right- and left-hand sides: add one triangle to the right by inserting the point on the right-hand side and leaving the other part of the triangle empty, then add a triangle to the left, inserting the point to the left and leaving the other part empty (see page 14. Proceed in the same way for the remaining rows, remembering to add the reverse triangles.

Row	15	16
Dark blue	2 + 4 + 4 + 4 + 2 side 1 + 1	2 + 3 + 3 + 3 + 2 side 1 + 1
White	1 + 1 + 1 + 1	2 + 2 + 2 + 2

Row	17
Dark blue	2 + 1 + 2 + 1 + 2 + 1 +2 + 1 + 2 side 1 + 1
White	1 + 1 + 1 + 1 + 1 + 1 + 1 + 1

Row	18
Dark blue	1 + 1+ 2 + 2 + 1 + 2 + 2 + 1 + 1 side 1 + 1
White	1 + 2 + 1 + 1 + 1 + 1 + 2 + 1

Row	19
Dark blue	1 + 3 + 1 + 1 + 2 + 1 + 1 + 3 + 1 side 1 + 1
White	2 + 1 + 1 + 1 + 1 + 1 + 1 + 2

Row	20
Dark blue	1 + 1 + 2 + 1 +1 + 1 + 1 + 2 + 1 + 1 side 1 + 1
White	1 + 1 + 2 + 2 + 1 + 2 + 2 + 1 + 1

At this point, do not increase the sides any more, but begin to create the peaks.

Start by inserting one light-blue to the right and one to the left and continue, using the table below.

Row	21
Dark blue	1 + 2 + 1 + 1 + 1 + 1 + 1 + 1 + 2 + 1
White	2 + 1 + 1 + 1 + 2 + 1 + 1 + 1 + 2

Now continue, not working in rows any more, but building each peak. At the centre of the two white triangles, insert one dark-blue triangle, add one to the right and one to the left of the one you have just inserted. You will then have three dark-blue triangles. In the centre of these, add another two dark-blue triangles and then one other dark-blue triangle in the middle of them, thus forming the first peak. Continue in this way, starting with the design made by the two white triangles with the one dark-blue one in the centre. Insert two white triangles, one dark-blue to the right and one dark-blue to the left after the blue triangle.

Insert one white triangle, one dark-blue to the right and one dark-blue to the left above the two white triangles. Insert two dark-blue triangles above the white one and one dark-blue triangle above them. In this way, you will complete the second peak.

Now move on to form the central peak, above the two white triangles and continue as follows:

- One dark-blue plus one white and two dark-blue to the right plus one white and two dark-blue to the left.
- Two dark-blue plus one white and one dark-blue to the right plus one white and one dark-blue to the left.
- One dark-blue plus one white and one dark-blue to the right, plus one white and one dark-blue to the left.
- Two white triangles plus one dark-blue to the right, plus one dark-blue to the left.
- One white triangle plus one dark-blue to the right, plus one dark-blue to the left.
- Two dark-blue.
- One dark-blue.

You have finished the central peak.

Repeat the instructions above for the second peak, and then the ones for the first, to complete the base of all the peaks.

Make the final round with one light-blue point and one dark-blue point of the triangles. Continue working upwards, taking the previous point together with the new one until you reach the last dark-blue point. Repeat on the right-hand side of the first peak; at the end you will find two light-blue triangles – insert another one to form the point.

Proceed in the same way on all the peaks until the swan's body is completed.

We recommend spraying the swan with transparent matt protective spray, two or three times at intervals. This protects the paper, and it can then also be dusted and cleaned more easily.

The swan is almost finished. To create the neck stack twenty-nine dark-blue triangles by inserting the points into each other and end with a light-blue triangle (see page 18). For the beak, create a smaller white triangle and stick it onto the point with a tiny bit of glue. Use a black marker to create eyes for your swan's head.

Yellow Penguin

Materials required:

7 blue triangles
50 red triangles
310 yellow triangles
1 orange triangle
Yellow felt

Googly eyes
Hat, straw or felt
Glue
Transparent matt
  protective spray

Prepare the triangles as explained in the *Technique* section (page 8), taking care with the folds. Continue with the rows as described in *Opening technique* (page 10).

Row	1–2	3	4	5	6	7	8
Yellow	20	20	20	14	15	14	15
Red				6	5	6	5

Row	9	10	11	12	13	14	15–16–17
Yellow	14	15	14	15	14	15	20
Red	6	5	6	5	4		
Blue					1 right + 1 left	5	

From the centre, skip a point and insert nineteen yellow triangles. Finish inserting all the triangles and press lightly inwards to give a more rounded form to the penguin, pressing on the last circle at the top to close it as much as possible.

We recommend spraying the work with transparent matt protective spray, two or three times at intervals. This protects the paper, and it can then also be dusted and cleaned more easily. This should be done before adding the finishing touches in felt or other materials.

Prepare two felt rectangles of 7.5 × 3cm (3 × 1¼in). Round off one short end, leaving the opposite side straight to form the flippers. Glue a flipper on each side of the body on the yellow triangles one the same row as the front blue triangles. With the same felt, make the bow tie and the feet and glue on – the bow tie under the blue row, and the feet under the body.

Make the beak with an orange triangle and glue to the centre of the face, onto the yellow triangles.

Glue on the eyes. Add a straw hat if you wish, which can be found in hobby and crafts shops, or make one yourself out of felt (see page 27).

Blue Penguin

Materials required:

310 blue triangles
115 white triangles
Yellow, black and white felt
Blue cardboard

Red and blue ribbon
Glue
Transparent matt protective spray

Prepare the triangles as explained in the *Technique* section (page 8), taking care with the folds. Continue with the rows as described in *Opening technique* (page 10).

Row	1–2	3	4	5	6	7	8
White	26	8	9	8	9	8	7
Blue		18	17	18	17	18	19

Row	9	10	11	12	13	14–16
White	6	5				
Blue	20	21	26	26	26	26

We recommend spraying the work with transparent matt protective spray, two or three times at intervals. This protects the paper, and it can then also be dusted and cleaned more easily. This should be done before adding the finishing touches in felt or other materials.

To complete the project, apply the eyes (I used black felt here, but you can use ready-made eyes if you wish).

Continue with the feet: cut two squares of yellow felt 2.5 × 2.5cm (1 × 1in), round off on one side and shape into toes on the other. Glue on the feet, one under the base and one on the front of the body, as shown in the photograph.

Create the beak with a yellow 2.5 × 1.5cm (1 × ½in) felt rectangle: cut it into an oval and glue it onto the face at the centre of the uppermost white row. Underneath glue on some red ribbon tied into a bow, if you wish.

For the flippers, take some blue card (or foam sheet, if you prefer), cut two ovals of about 4 × 2.5cm (1½ × 1in). Glue the flippers into gaps between the blue triangles on both sides of the body. Cut a white felt circle that is slightly larger than the hole on the penguin's head and glue it on.

For the hat, cut out an 8cm (3¼in) diameter circle from white felt, make a cut into the centre and remove 2mm of felt to create a slice. Stick either side of the slice with glue, slightly overlapping, to create a cone. Press lightly on the wider part to make a pointed shape and complete by applying coordinating ribbon. Glue the hat at a slight angle on top of the penguin.

Tortoise

Materials required:

60 yellow triangles
30 red triangles
Glue

Transparent matt
protective spray
Black marker

Prepare the triangles as explained in the *Technique* section (page 8), taking care with the folds. Unlike the other projects, you will not work in circles for the yellow tortoise but flat.

Proceed as follows:

- Take three yellow triangles and hook above another two yellow triangles, leaving the two outer points free.
- Insert one yellow triangle to the right on the two outer points, inserting the point onto the left-hand pocket, then one yellow triangle to the left, inserting the point into the pocket on the right.
- Insert three yellow triangles, leaving the outer points free.
- Insert one red triangle to the right on the two outer points, inserting the point onto the left-hand pocket, then one red triangle to the left, inserting the point into the pocket on the right.
- Insert four yellow triangles, leaving the outer points free.
- Insert one red triangle to the right on the two outer points, inserting the point onto the left-hand pocket, then one red triangle to the left, inserting the point into the pocket on the right.
- Insert five yellow triangles, leaving the outer points free.
- Insert one red triangle to the right on the two outer points, inserting the point onto the left-hand pocket, then one red triangle to the left, inserting the point into the pocket on the right.

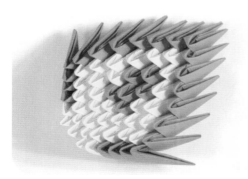

- Insert six triangles (two yellow plus two red plus two yellow) leaving the outer points free.
- Insert one red triangle to the right on the two outer points, inserting the point onto the left-hand pocket, then one red triangle to the left, inserting the point into the pocket on the right.
- Insert five triangles (two yellow plus one red plus two yellow), leaving the outer points free.

You will have two points to the right and two points to the left.

- Insert one red triangle into each side.
- Insert six triangles (one red plus one yellow plus two red plus one yellow plus one red) leaving the outer points free.
- Insert five triangles (one red plus one yellow plus one red plus one yellow plus one red) leaving the outer points free.
- Insert three triangles (one red plus one yellow plus one red) leaving the outer points free.
- Insert two red triangles, leaving the outer points free.
- Insert one red triangle, leaving the outer points free.

The tortoise shell is now complete.

For the legs:

Make four stacks of three yellow triangles (see page 18).

For the head:

Stack three yellow triangles on top of a red, as shown. Fit the stack onto the central triangle of the first circle, inserting the two points.

Insert one yellow triangle in the centre and one on the right into the reverse pockets, inserting a point into the yellow triangle you have just placed and the other point into the straight yellow triangle. Continue with one yellow triangle to the left-hand side, inserting a point into the yellow triangle that has just been inserted and the other point into the straight yellow triangle. End by adding one yellow reverse triangle at the top into the two available pockets.

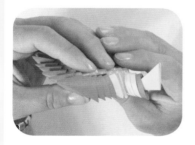  

  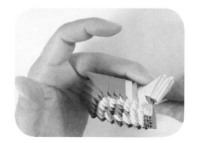

Attaching the legs:

Take one red triangle and insert one left-hand point into the first triangle to the right of the head, and glue. In the same way, insert the right-hand point into the first triangle on the left, and glue. Leave to dry and then insert the free point into a leg. Attach the other front leg in the same way.

  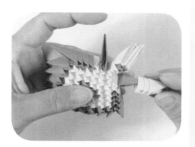

To position the back legs, glue a yellow point inside the fourth side red triangle, counting from the bottom. Leave to dry and insert the other point into one of the legs you have made. Repeat on the opposite side.

Again we recommend spraying the work with transparent matt protective spray, two or three times at intervals.

With a black marker pen, draw the eyes on the sides of the head.

Owl

Materials required:

110 green triangles
130 white triangles
360 pink triangles
60 blue triangles

7 yellow triangles
Eyes
Transparent matt protective spray

Prepare the triangles as explained in the *Technique* section (page 8), taking care with the folds. Continue with the rows as described in *Opening technique* (page 10).

Row	1–2	3	4	5
Green	18	18 reverse	18 reverse	10 reverse
Pink				8

Continue now, working on the back only, as follows:

- Above the pink triangles, insert seven blue triangles plus two pink triangles to the side, plus nine reverse green triangles.
- Skip a point and insert eight pink triangles above the blue ones.
- Skip a point and insert one pink triangle plus five blue triangles plus one pink triangle.
- Skip a point and insert six pink triangles.
- Skip a point and insert one pink triangle plus three blue triangles plus one pink triangle.
- Skip a point and insert four pink triangles; above these insert three pink triangles, and above these insert two pink triangles and finish with one pink triangle.
- Continue now from the bottom right, starting with a green/pink point and insert one reverse blue triangle. Carry on upwards, taking one point you have just placed and insert another eight reverse blue triangles.
- Repeat the previous step on the left-hand side.
- End with a blue triangle at the top.
- Insert one reverse blue triangle to the right plus one reverse blue triangle to the left, at the bottom, above the green.

Now move to the front:

- Above the green triangles, insert six green reverse triangles.
- Above again, now insert five green reverse triangles.
- One reverse blue triangle above, a blue/green point to the right and one to the left.
- * One pink straight triangle in the middle of the blue ones.
- * Two pink straight triangles above the previous pink one.
- Repeat the two rows marked with * on the other side.
- One straight blue triangle on a blue point.
- One reverse white triangle on a green point.
- Three straight yellow triangles each hooked onto a single point (three yellows = three points).
- Two white reverse triangles each hooked onto a single point (two whites = two points).
- Three yellow straight triangles each hooked onto a single point (three yellow = three points).
- One white reverse triangle on a green point.
- One straight blue triangle on a blue point.
- Starting with the white, insert nine reverse white triangles.
- Continue with eight reverse white triangles.
- Rising again, continue with 7–6–5–4–3–2 white reverse triangles.
- Starting from the bottom upwards, insert eight straight blue triangles on the two white sides, taking the point of the triangle that has just been inserted.
- Continue on the top with three straight white triangles.
- Above these, three white straight triangles.
- Now start with the pink side and above the two pink straight triangles, insert three triangles, four triangles, five triangles, six triangles, seven triangles, eight triangles, nine triangles (all straight pink).
- Repeat on the opposite side.

- Now continue for another two rounds with pink straight triangles until you are in line with the four white triangles inserted previously.
- Go back to the white and insert five straight white and twenty straight pink triangles.
- Go back to the white and insert six straight white and nineteen straight pink triangles.
- Go back to the white and insert seven straight white and eighteen straight pink triangles.
- Go back to the white and insert eight reverse white and seventeen straight pink triangles.
- In the middle of the white, insert one straight yellow triangle.
- Continue by inserting four white reverse triangles to the right, plus four white reverse triangles to the left.
- Complete the circle with sixteen straight pink triangles.
- Above the white triangles, leave one point and insert eight white reverse triangles plus seventeen straight pink triangles.
- Above the yellow, insert one straight pink triangle plus four reverse white triangles, plus four reverse white triangles to the left plus sixteen straight pink triangles.

- Above the pink, insert two pink reverse triangles plus four white reverse triangles to the right, plus four white reverse triangles to the left plus fifteen pink reverse triangles.
- Above the two pink triangles, insert three pink straight triangles and end the circle with pink reverse triangles.
- ** Now prepare the two sides separately. Begin from the right-hand side and insert one straight pink triangle plus three white reverse triangles plus one reverse pink triangle.
- Above, continue with one straight pink triangle plus three pink reverse triangles.
- End with one pink straight triangle close to the straight triangle from the previous circle.
- Repeat from ** on the opposite side.
- Now complete the rear with two full rounds of pink reverse triangles.

We recommend spraying the owl with transparent matt protective spray, two or three times at intervals. This should be done before adding the finishing touches in felt or other materials.

To complete the piece, add the eyes.

Squirrel

Materials required:

150 white triangles
390 brown triangles
100 black triangles

Glue
Googly eyes
Transparent matt
   protective spray

Prepare the triangles as explained in the *Technique* section (page 8), taking care with the folds. Continue with the rows as described in *Opening technique* (page 10).

Row	1–2	3	4	5	6	7	8
White		6	7	6	7	6	7
Brown	22	16	6	6	6	6	6
Black			1 + 1	4	1 + 1	4	1 + 1
Brown			1 + 6	6	1 + 6	6	1 + 6

Row	9	10	11	12	13	14	15	16
White	6	7	6	7	6	7	6	7
Brown	6	6	6	6	6	6	6	6
Black	4	1 + 1	4	1 + 1	4	1 + 1	4	1 + 1
Brown	6	1 + 6	6	1 + 6	6	1 + 6	6	1 + 6

Work with the following charts above. For row 17, starting with the white, insert the triangles by taking three points – two in one pocket and one in the other – (see *Decreasing*, page 15).

Row	17	18	19	20	21	22	23	24
White	5		5 reverse	4	3 + 1 black*	2		
Brown	10	15 reverse	10 reverse	5	5	6	13	14
Black				1	2	1	2	1
Brown				5	5	6		

* In the centre of the white area, insert one black triangle above to form the nose.

For the ears:

From the centre front (where the mouth is), leave two triangles and insert three brown triangles reverse and another two brown triangles over them. Repeat the same on the opposite side.

To create the tail:

Take three brown triangles, insert one black triangle and one white triangle above, and insert two brown triangles on the sides, inserting the point from the previous round into the outermost pocket of the triangle.

Continue by inserting the triangles as described below for each row:

- Two black plus one white.
- One black plus one white plus two brown at sides.
- One white plus two brown at sides.
- One black plus one white plus two brown at sides.
- Two black plus one white.
- One black plus one white plus two brown at sides.
- One black plus two white.
- Two black plus two brown at sides.
- One black plus two white.
- Two black plus two brown at sides.
- One white plus one black plus one white.
- One white plus one black plus two brown at sides.
- One white plus two black.
- One white plus one black plus two brown at sides.
- One white plus two black.
- One white plus one black plus two brown at sides.
- One white plus two black.
- Two white plus two brown at sides.
- Two black plus one white.
- One black plus one white plus two brown at sides.
- Two black plus one white.

- Two black plus two brown at sides.
- Two black plus one white.
- Two white plus two brown at sides.
- Two black plus one white.
- Two white plus two brown at sides.
- Insert one white triangle in the brown side and two black triangles above.
- Insert one white triangle plus two brown in the first black.
- Repeat the last two stages on the opposite side too.

Then start from the left-hand side of the tail in the following way.

- One brown plus two black plus one white plus two black plus one brown.
- One brown plus one black plus two white plus one black plus one brown.
- One brown plus one black plus one white plus one black plus one brown.
- One brown plus two black plus one brown.
- One brown plus one black plus one brown.
- Two brown.

To attach the tail, take two new brown triangles and glue them by putting the closed point into a pocket on the side of the body, between the two black rows at the back. Leave to dry and insert the previously prepared tail on the two points, with a spot of glue. Leave to dry again and then shape it with your hands as you desire.

We recommend spraying the squirrel with transparent matt protective spray, two or three times at intervals. This protects the paper, and it can then also be dusted and cleaned more easily. This should be done before adding the finishing touches in felt or other materials.

To complete the piece, glue on the eyes.

Panda

Materials required:

480 white triangles
220 black triangles
Black and white felt

Glue
Transparent matt protective spray
Nose

Prepare the triangles as explained in the *Technique* section (page 8), taking care with the folds. Continue with the rows as described in *Opening technique* (page 10).

Row	1–2	3–8	9	10	11	12	13
White	23	23	7	6	5	4	
Black			16	17	18	19	23

Row	14	15
White		
Black	23	23

To continue with the head, insert a black triangle between the two pockets of the previous triangle, keeping the straight part perpendicular and the long side on top as in the photo below. As it will not support itself, place some glue on the triangle before adding it.

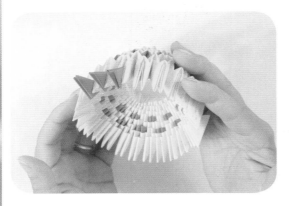

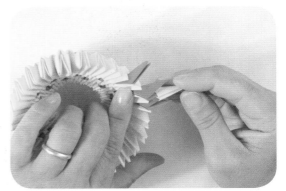

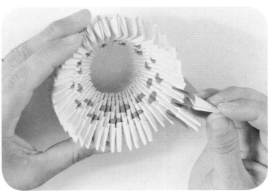

In these three stages, the red/yellow triangles have been used to show the steps, on rows 16 and 17, more clearly. On the panda, these two rows are made using black triangles only.

Rows 16 and 17: Complete the whole row with black triangles. Then insert one white reverse triangle, taking one point to the right and one to the left. Complete the row. Continue with the table below using straight triangles.

Row	18	19	20
White	23	23	23

Identify the centre front and insert two whites to the right and two to the left, thus giving you four triangles. Insert three white triangles above and another two white triangles over them.

Continue by adding the number of triangles as below to complete each row.

Row	21	22	23	24	25	26	27
Black	3 + 3	4 + 4	5 + 5	4 + 4	5 + 5	4 + 4	3 + 3
White	13	12	11	12 + 3	11 + 2	12 + 3	13 + 4

Continue with another three rounds, all white.

We recommend spraying the panda with transparent matt protective spray, two to three times at intervals. This protects the paper, and it can then also be dusted and cleaned more easily. This should be done before adding the finishing touches in felt or other materials.

Prepare two 1.5cm (½in) white felt circles for the eyes. Glue a small black circle in the middle of each. Glue the eyes onto the black triangles.

Create two 5cm (2in) diameter circles of black felt (trim off a small part) and glue on the two sides at the top, to make the ears. For the nose, use a ready-made one, or use a small oval piece of black felt. For the arms, cut out and glue two long 5 × 4cm (2 × 1½in) rectangles of black felt, rounded off on one side, and place them on the panda's sides. For feet, use two 3 × 2.5cm (1¼ × 1in) triangles, rounding them more on one side to give the shape of a paw. Glue them onto the white triangles at the bottom.

To finish, create the mouth with a small strip of black felt.

White Rabbit

Materials required:

465 white triangles

115 red triangles

12 blue triangles

Black beads for eyes and nose

Glue

Red pearl bead

Felt butterfly

Transparent matt protective spray

Prepare the triangles as explained in the *Technique* section (page 8), taking care with the folds. Continue with the rows as described in *Opening technique* (page 10).

Row	1–2	3	4	5	6	7	8
White	24	24 reverse	24 reverse				
Red				24	24	24	24

Row	9	10
Blue	12	
Red	12	
White		24 reverse

To form the head, take the number of triangles from twenty-four to thirty-two, and to do this insert empty triangles (see *Increasing*, page 13). Then continue following the chart below.

Row	11	12	13	14	15	16	17
White	32	32	32	32	32	32	32

For the ears:

Holding the rabbit in front of you with the blue row at the front, identify the centre and count seven triangles to the left from this point, then insert seven white reverse triangles. Leave four triangles and insert another seven reverse triangles. Continue with the ears, with reverse triangles added as follows: rows of six, then five on top, then six on top, then five, then six, then five, then six, then five, then four and then three to finish.

Repeat the same for the other ear.

We recommend spraying the rabbit with transparent matt protective spray, two or three times at intervals. This protects the paper, and it can then also be dusted and cleaned more easily. This should be done before adding the finishing touches in felt or other materials.

Glue a small red pearl bead in the centre of the blue triangles, then three rows above this – on the white – apply a small black bead for the nose and on the row above, to the left and right of the nose, attach the eyes. Place a blue butterfly or a flower near the ears if you wish.

Finally, create the arms:

Fold a 10 × 5cm (4 × 2in) red rectangle in the usual way, then open it up and fold the right point and then close it again. Make two. Prepare two normal-sized white triangles in the same way, fold the point and close. Insert a white triangle into a large red one and then place it in a gap between two blue triangles on the body, keeping the longer part at the top.

Repeat to attach the other arm.

Frog

Materials required:

290 green triangles
80 white triangles
2 black pearls

Glue
Transparent matt protective spray

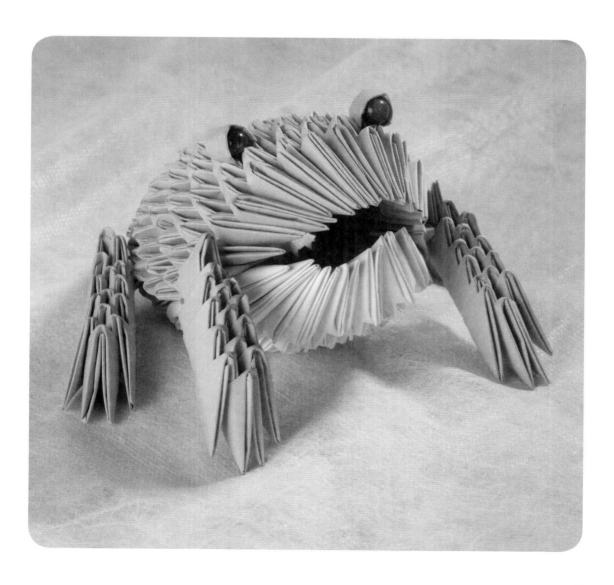

Prepare the triangles as explained on page 8, taking care with the folds. Do not make the normal opening circle for the frog, but do the following instead:

- Take six green triangles and hook five green triangles above them, leaving the first and the last point free.
- Insert one green triangle per side on these.
- Continue by inserting six green triangles above them.
- Above these, insert seven green triangles, taking the point from the previous round.
- Then insert six green triangles and add two green triangles onto the side points.
- Seven green triangles plus two green triangles on the side points.
- Eight green triangles plus two green triangles on the side points.
- Nine green triangles plus two green triangles on the side points.
- Ten green triangles plus two green triangles on the side points.
- Eleven green triangles plus two green triangles on the side points.

Now put the piece to one side. Take seven white triangles, hook six white triangles above them and then another five white triangles.

Join the first of the seven white triangles with one of the top row of the green triangles, joining them with a green triangle, and then carry on marrying up the two sections using one white triangle and one green triangle.

Carry out this same step on the other side.

You will now have a circle on which to continue your work, inserting:

- Twelve green triangles, starting with the green, plus eight white triangles starting from the white.
- Thirteen green triangles plus seven white triangles.
- Continue with the white only and insert six white triangles and another five white triangles above.
- Leave the first point of the green ones and insert twelve green triangles.
- Continue by leaving one point free and inserting eleven green triangles plus one green triangle to the right and one to the left, taking the point from the previous circle.
- Now insert one green triangle on each side, taking one green point and two white points.
- Continue by adding six white triangles plus fourteen green triangles.
- Then add seven white triangles plus thirteen green triangles.
- Continue with white only, inserting six.
- Insert another seven white triangles above them.
- Without joining them to the white, continue with the green and insert twelve green triangles.
- Insert eleven green triangles above them.
- Insert nine green triangles above them.
- Complete by inserting eight green triangles.

Using your fingers inside the shape, make it slightly rounder and press the top and bottom to bring the mouth closer.

Now make the frog's legs:

- One green triangle.
- Insert two green triangles above this.
- Insert one green triangle above these.
- Insert two green triangles above this.
- Insert one green triangle above these.
- Insert two green triangles above this.
- Insert one green triangle above these.
- Insert two green triangles above this.
- End with one green triangle on top.

Make all four legs in this way (see also *Creating long elements*, page 19).

To attach the legs to the body, glue a new open triangle between the green and white of the mouth, inserting one point inside and keeping the other outside, with the longer part behind and the point in front. Prepare both inserts in this way for the front legs. For the back legs, repeat as above, inserting the point on the side on the seventh row and inserting the open triangle with the point facing the back and the straight part in front. Before gluing the attachments, check them all, as they can't be separated once they are stuck together. Insert the point now sticking out into the inner side of the legs. Insert two triangles and once you have checked it is correct, glue them. Repeat for all four legs. Leave to dry.

Now insert two green triangles, one above the other, behind each leg, in the triangle that juts out most. Continue with one triangle, placing one point into the triangle you have just inserted and the other on the inner side. Proceed in the same way for all legs.

We recommend spraying the frog with transparent matt protective spray, two or three times at intervals. This protects the paper, and it can then also be dusted and cleaned more easily. This should be done before adding the finishing touches.

To add the eyes, take a green rectangle, fold it along its length into three parts to make a strip, and insert one bead with a spot of glue. Pinch at the bottom to close in the bead, leave about 1cm (½in) each side and cut off the excess. Fold down to form a triangle and glue everything in the centre of the third row leaving about three triangles between one eye and the other.

White Cat

Materials required:

450 white triangles

120 black triangles

A bell and a piece of waxed cord

Glue

Googly eyes

Black bead for nose

Transparent matt protective spray

Prepare the triangles as explained in the *Technique* section (page 8), taking care with the folds. Continue with the rows as described in *Opening technique* (page 10).

Row	1–2	3	4	5	6	7	8
White	22	22	22	22	6 + 12	7 + 13	22
Black					2 + 2	1 + 1	

Row	9	10
White	22	22

On row 11, it is necessary to increase the triangles to twenty-eight (see *Increasing*, page 13), using the black triangles.

Row	11	12	13	14	15
White			28	26	28
Black	28 reverse	28 reverse		2 + 2 white*	

* To create the mouth, insert two straight black triangles and one white triangle above them, as if it were a double triangle.

Row	16	17	18	19
White	28	28	7 central	5 central
Black			21	3 right + 3 left
White				17

For the ears:

- Position them above the three black triangles.
- Insert two white triangles.
- Continue with one black plus one white plus one black.
- Insert two white triangles.
- Finish with one black triangle.
- Repeat on the opposite side to form the other ear.

For the tail:

- Insert two white triangles above one black triangle.
- One black triangle.
- Two white triangles, taking the points of the previous white triangles.
- One black triangle.
- Two white triangles, taking the points of the previous white triangles.
- One black triangle.

- Two white triangles, taking the points of the previous white triangles.
- Three black triangles.
- Two white triangles.
- Three black triangles.

For the paws:

- Insert two white triangles above one black triangle.
- One black triangle.
- Two white triangles, taking the points of the previous white triangles.
- One black triangle.
- Two white triangles, taking the points of the previous white triangles.
- One black triangle in the centre plus two white triangles on the side.
- Two white triangles.
- Prepare three smaller black triangles and insert them, joining the six top points, two at a time.

Prepare the other paw in the same way.

To attach the tail, take a new black triangle, insert the closed point into the pocket in the centre of the body at the back and glue. Leave to dry and insert the previously prepared tail on the two points, with a spot of glue.

Attach the paws in the same way, inserting the triangle on the last white row of the body, parallel with the black triangle on the side.

We recommend spraying the cat with transparent matt protective spray, two or three times at intervals. This protects the paper, and it can then also be dusted and cleaned more easily. This should be done before adding the finishing touches.

To complete the piece, add the nose just above the mouth. You should glue on the whiskers first, which are made by cutting four pieces of black waxed cord. Stick on the eyes, a row or two above the nose. As further embellishment, I used a black collar made from waxed cord with a bell attached.

Brown Dog

Materials required:

- 680 beige triangles
- 135 white triangles.
- 60 black triangles
- 30 brown triangles
- 1 red triangle
- Black foam sheet
- Glue
- Googly eyes
- Black bead for nose
- Transparent matt protective spray

Prepare the triangles as explained in the *Technique* section (page 8), taking care with the folds. Continue with the rows described below, as per *Creating a closed base* (page 16).

Row	1–2	3	4	5	6	7	8
Black							1
Brown				3 + 3	1 + 1	1	1
White						3	1
Black					1 + 1		
Beige	23	23	23	8 + 9	10 + 9	4 + 11	5 + 12
White						3	
Brown						1	1
White							1
Black							1

Row	9	10	11	12	13	14	15–16
Black	3	3	2	3	4		
Brown	1	2	3	1	2		
White	1			3	6	23	
Black							
Beige	4 + 9	5 + 8	6 + 7	3 + 6	0 + 5		23 reverse
White	1			3			
Brown	1	2	3	1	2		
White							
Black	3	3	2	3	4		

Follow the chart above. Then insert seven beige triangles in the centre as in the photo below, attaching them with glue.

Continue with one row of reverse beige triangles, increasing the triangles from twenty-three to twenty-eight. Make the increases to the front of the piece. The triangles inserted above the reverse ones will not be the same as the rest of the piece, therefore work on the front of the face separately until the instructions tell you to join it to the rest of the project.

Front face:

One full circle of beige straight triangles. Centre front, insert one white triangle into the gap to the right between the two colours and hook them with two white triangles. Insert another white triangle into the left gap and hook with two whites, then insert two whites to the right and two to the left.

- In the middle, five whites plus two beige to the right and two to the left.
- In the middle, six whites plus two beige to the right and two to the left.
- In the middle, five whites plus one beige to the right and one to the left.
- In the middle, one white plus one red plus one white and two beige to the right and two to the left.
- In the middle, two whites plus two beige to the right and two to the left.
- In the middle, three whites plus two beige to the right and two to the left.
- In the middle, four whites plus two beige to the right and two to the left.

Continue with all the beige rows at the back until you reach the same level as the front of the face.

- Insert one beige triangle to the right on top and one to the left, to join the back triangles with the front ones.
- Insert seven reverse triangles to the front, skip one point and complete the entire circle with straight beige triangles.
- Insert eight white reverse triangles above the previous ones overlapping, plus two straight beige to the right and three straight beige to the left.
- Insert seven white reverse triangles above the previous ones overlapping, plus two straight beige to the right and two straight beige to the left.
- Continue above this with nine straight beige triangles.
- Continue above this again with eight straight beige triangles.
- For the back part, count the rows and complete twelve rows even if not in line.

For the ears:

- Work on the dog from the back and, starting from the left, complete one ear at a time.
- Insert six black reverse triangles.
- Skip one point and insert one black plus three white, plus one reverse black above.
- Skip one point and insert one beige plus one white plus black plus one reverse beige.
- Taking the point of the previous circle, insert two beige plus one black plus two reverse beige.
- Skip a point and insert four reverse beige.
- Skip a point and insert three reverse beige.
- Skip a point and insert two reverse beige.

Repeat everything for the other ear, starting from the right.

Once the second ear is complete, insert three straight beige triangles between the ears, two straight beige triangles above those and one straight beige triangle above those.

For the front legs:

- Two beige triangles.
- Above these, three beige triangles.
- Above these again, two beige triangles.
- Above these, one beige plus one white plus one beige.
- Complete with two black.
- Repeat these steps to create the other leg.

For the back legs:

- Three beige triangles.
- Above these, two beige triangles.
- Above these, three beige triangles.
- Above these, two white triangles.
- Finish with one black triangle.
- Repeat for the other leg.

Now adjust the two legs to form one left and one right. For the right: at the top, above the three beige triangles, insert one beige triangle to the right. Then insert another beige triangle into the one you have just positioned, taking the point of the previous circle. Continue by inserting another beige triangle above the one you have just inserted. By doing so, the leg will shift to the right. For the left: repeat the instructions above, working to the left side (rather than right).

For the tail:

Stack six beige triangles plus one smaller black triangle one above the other. To attach the tail, take a new beige triangle and insert the closed point into the pocket in the centre of the body behind, on the second row, then glue. Leave to dry and insert the previously prepared tail on the two points, with a spot of glue.

To attach the front legs:

On the front, underneath the white triangles, glue on two triangles 1cm (½in) apart, leaving the reverse points out, and insert another two on the opposite side. Wait for them to dry and insert the points into the front legs with a spot of glue (test them first without the glue).

To attach the back legs:

Create a smaller triangle, glue one part into the first triangle at the top of the leg (pay attention to left and right – the leg must adhere to the body). Then, when dry, insert the other part of the triangle into the pocket on the third row, leaving three triangles from the tail. Leave to dry. Position the leg to check it is correct. Attach the inner part, bent towards the body, with the glue. Repeat for the other back leg.

Before completing the project, we recommend spraying the dog with transparent matt protective spray, two or three times at intervals. This protects the paper, and it can then also be dusted and cleaned more easily. This should be done before adding the finishing touches.

To complete the dog, attach the nose and the eyes.

For the collar:

Take a strip of black foam sheet, 30 × 0.5cm (11¾ × ¼in) long, and glue red sequins onto it. Place around the dog's neck to create a collar and glue at the back, cutting off the excess.

Chick

Materials required:

102 yellow triangles

Yellow, orange, white and black felt

Glue

Transparent matt protective spray

Prepare the triangles as explained in the *Technique* section (page 8), taking care with the folds. Continue with the rows as described in *Opening technique* (page 10).

Row	1–2	3	4	5	6	7	8	9	10
Yellow	10	10	10	10	10	10	10	10	10

Make the chick in accordance with the chart. Before continuing your project, we recommend spraying the piece with protective transparent matt spray, two or three times at intervals. This protects the paper, and it can then also be dusted and cleaned more easily. This should be done before adding the final touches in felt or other materials.

To complete the chick, glue two triangles onto row 6, inserted into a side pocket to create the wings. Make the eyes with white and black felt and glue between the two wings. Make the feet with orange felt 2 × 1.5cm (¾ × ½in), rounding them on one side and creating toes on the other. Cut out a diamond shape of 2 × 1cm (¾ × ⅜in) for the beak.

Also make a 3cm (1¼in) diameter, yellow felt circle and another one with a 5cm (2in) diameter. Shape these as in the photograph opposite. Stick the largest to the chick's head, gluing it onto the triangles. Apply the other to the bottom part to close the hole. Once this has been stuck down, add the red feet, bringing the points outwards.

To finish, glue the beak between the eyes.

Blue

Rabbit

Materials required:

280 light-blue triangles

26 larger
  light-blue triangles

20 dark-blue triangles

White and black felt

Black bead for nose

Glue

Transparent matt
  protective spray

repare the triangles as explained in the *Technique* section (page 8), taking care with the folds. Continue with the rows described below, as per *Creating a closed base* (page 16). To close the base completely, the triangles used for it must be larger than usual, so make twenty-six 8 × 6cm (3¼ × 2½in) triangles; the inner angle will be smaller during folding.

Row	1–2	3	4	5	6	7	8	9
Light Blue	26	26	26	26	26	26	26	26

To make this head piece stronger, it is possible to stick on row 9 by placing a small amount of glue on the points of the previous line.

Use reverse triangles to create the ears:

- Insert four light-blue triangles (as the piece up to this point is all the same, you can begin from any point).
- Above this, insert one light-blue triangle plus one dark-blue plus one light-blue.
- Continue, taking a point from the previous circle, and insert one light-blue plus two dark-blue plus one light-blue.
- One light-blue plus one dark-blue plus one light-blue.
- Continue, taking a point from the previous circle, and insert one light-blue plus two dark-blue plus one light-blue.
- One light-blue plus one dark-blue plus one light-blue.
- Continue, taking a point from the previous circle and insert one light-blue plus two dark-blue plus one light-blue.
- One light-blue plus one dark-blue plus one light-blue.
- Leave the two side points and insert two light-blue.

To make the other ear, leave four points free from the bottom moving right, and insert four reverse light-blue.

Continue as above and complete the second ear.

Before finishing your project, we recommend spraying the rabbit with transparent matt protective spray, two or three times at intervals. This protects the paper, and it can then also be dusted and cleaned more easily. This should be done before adding the finishing touches in felt or other materials.

To complete your project, glue on the nose and eyes (here, instead of using ready-made eyes, I used black and white felt).

The rabbit can be used as a pencil pot.

Yellow Cat

Materials required:

310 yellow triangles
26 larger yellow triangles
8 brown triangles
White and black felt
Black bead for nose

White waxed cord
Glue
Transparent matt
  protective spray

repare the triangles as explained in the *Technique* section
(page 8), taking care with the folds. Continue with the rows
described below, as per *Creating a closed base* (page 16). To
close the base completely, the triangles used to create it must
be larger, so make twenty-six 8 × 6cm (3¼ × 2½in) triangles;
the inner angle will be smaller during folding.

Row	1–2	3	4	5	6	7	8	9–11
Yellow	26	26	26	26	26	26	26	26

To make this piece stronger, it is possible to stick down
row 11 by placing a small amount of glue on the points of the
previous line.

For the ears:

- Insert two yellow triangles (as the piece is all the same up to
  now, you can start from any point) plus one brown triangle
  plus two yellow triangles.
- Above, insert one yellow triangle plus two brown plus
  one yellow.
- Above these, one yellow plus one brown plus one yellow.
- Continue with two yellow.
- Complete with one yellow.

To make the other ear, leave four points free from the bottom
moving right, and insert two yellow plus one brown plus
two yellow.

Continue as above and complete the second ear.

Before completing your project, we recommend spraying the
piece with transparent matt protective spray, two or three times
at intervals. This protects the paper, and it can then also be
dusted and cleaned more easily. This should be done before
adding the finishing touches in felt or other materials.

To complete the piece, glue on the nose and ears (here I used
black and white felt instead of ready-made eyes). Add two
pieces of white waxed cord to create whiskers before applying
the nose.

The cat can be used as a pencil pot.

Spotty Dog

Materials required:

225 white triangles

26 larger white triangles

65 brown triangles

White and black felt

Black bead for nose

Glue

Transparent matt protective spray